# Word Songs and Whimsies

# Word Songs and Whimsies

*A Nest of Poems and Verse*

RAYMOND H. HAAN

RESOURCE *Publications* · Eugene, Oregon

WORD SONGS AND WHIMSIES
A Nest of Poems and Verse

Copyright © 2020 Raymond H. Haan. All rights reserved. Except for brief quotations in critical publications or reviews, no part of this book may be reproduced in any manner without prior written permission from the publisher. Write: Permissions, Wipf and Stock Publishers, 199 W. 8th Ave., Suite 3, Eugene, OR 97401.

Resource Publications
An Imprint of Wipf and Stock Publishers
199 W. 8th Ave., Suite 3
Eugene, OR 97401

www.wipfandstock.com

PAPERBACK ISBN: 978-1-7252-6619-3
HARDCOVER ISBN: 978-1-7252-6617-9
EBOOK ISBN: 978-1-7252-6618-6

Manufactured in the U.S.A.    05/12/20

Dedicated
to the memory of my father,
Rev. Raymond H. Haan,
beloved in part for his loving use of words

# Contents

*Acknowledgement* | ix
*Introduction* | xi

Word Song | 1
Willingness | 2
Carpenter's Hands | 3
Solomon Sky | 4
Counterparts | 5
Psychology 101 | 6
The Victim | 7
Partly Subliminal | 8
Accessory to the Crimes | 9
Cleansing | 10
Vexation | 11
The Climb | 12
The Curse | 13
Paradigms | 14
Like a Duck | 15
Flowering Crab | 16
Faith | 17
Opportunity | 18
Laughing Buddha | 19
Cremation after All | 20
Invasive Species | 23
Mountain | 24
Enticement | 25
Nellie Tibble | 26
Recreation Comes to
  Michigan | 27
The Party Line | 28
Homage to "The Red
  Wheelbarrow" | 29
A Question for Flag Haters | 30

Maranatha | 31
West Ward | 32
Handicapped | 34
Petunias Bunched in the
  Sidewalk Crack | 35
Pine Rest Chapel,
  1929—2019 | 36
Liz | 38
Sundown | 39
Tree Huggers | 40
Sunflower Field I | 41
South End Reporter | 42
The Shade | 43
Invitation | 44
Suitability | 45
Crescent Moon Rising | 46
Ecclesiastical Cricket | 47
The Unfathomable Theology
  of Fishing | 48
Royce | 49
Robinical Example | 51
Sunflower Field II | 52
One by One | 53
Avian Diplomacy | 54
Arroyo | 55
Dwelling Place | 56
November Rose | 57
Immanuel | 58
Addiction | 60
Ocular Oxymoron | 61
Solace at Solstice | 62
Seasonal Spirit | 63
Transport | 64

# Acknowledgement

EMILY DICKINSON LIKENED BOOKS to frigates. This frigate might never have sailed without the enthusiastic encouragement of Dr. John Van Dyk or without the careful trimming of the sails by Kathleen Herrema. I am most grateful to each of them for helping to set this little craft on its voyage.

# Introduction
## *Anatomy, Personality, and Parentage*

POEMS RESEMBLE PEOPLE. Most obviously, poems have physical shapes. The shape of any poem contributes to its personality and also to our memory of it. Looking at the shapes of some poems, the reader directly knows their family names: sonnet, haiku, ballad stanza, limerick, cinquain, and others. Each family enjoys a unique shape—a genetic, predictable, and generally tidy figure. Free verse, having no defined form, meets the eye as an amorphous printed creature. When it gathers length, free verse sprawls across the page like a prodigious, inky amoeba. Regardless of the details, each poem has its own physical shape, just as people do.

Poems also have distinctive personalities, ranging from light-hearted to somber. Since part of any poem's personality derives from its insight or wisdom, we respect that poem in the measure that we perceive its insight—and, of course, to the extent that we agree with it. Poems with less wisdom we value for their attributes of joy, humor, music, or imagery—just as we love people for various reasons.

Quite obviously, every poem has a parent, its source of life and personality. In overt or subtle ways a poem offers information about its parent, and as a consequence, the parent faces interesting considerations. How much introspection, how much history, how much idiosyncrasy should a parent reveal? And why should any reader find one fragment of that to be interesting?

Like others of their kind, the poems between these covers have shape, personality, and parentage. So, if you choose, you may imagine each poem to be a synthetic person, having the potential for dislike and disregard or for affinity and friendship. Of course, the parent of the present poems hopes that you will make happy or thoughtful acquaintance with at least a few of his printed progeny.

## *Word Song*

A poem
is a word song
of truth, ever aching

to sing
from the word cage
its maker is making.

## *Willingness*

"Well, we've got five pregnant nannies," said farmer Linus,
"so we'll have plenty of milk in a few months.
But the billy we borrowed has to go.
He's obstinate, and he's been butting down fences.
I'm not sure I would get up if he butted me
with those eighteen-inch horns.
We can't keep a stubborn, temperamental animal like that."

Of course, I had to agree.
But it felt vaguely unfair,
for without the services of Grumpy Billy
we would have no milk—
and no frisky kids for a new generation.

But who would blame Billy for being grumpy?
Though his service here was good and necessary,
he had probably hated to come.
(After all, this wasn't *his* idea, his mission.)
He was probably content with his own pasture,
happy with his own sweet nannies.
Who knows? Maybe he didn't approve of Linus and Nancy,
maybe he thought their barn or their hay stank,
maybe these new nannies didn't behave right,
or maybe he just didn't like their style.

Anyway, it is sad that Billy is grumpy and stubborn,
sad that he rejects Linus's authority,
and sad that his crabbiness mutes
the joy we might take in him.

Yet, maybe I'll drink a glass of milk to Grumpy Billy
when it comes fresh from his harem,
and I'll ruminate on Grumpy Billy's mission—
how it extends beyond his own pen and pasture and natural desires—
just as Jonah's did.

## *Carpenter's Hands*

Rough and hard were the hands of the Carpenter,
worker with wood and stone, toiler with Joseph.
Rough and hard they must have been
from shaping, fitting, and maybe quarrying obdurate rocks
or from sawing, smoothing, and nailing
door frames, tables, yokes, or ploughs.
From the substance of His own creation
the Carpenter crafted things beautiful in usefulness,
crafted them with calloused hands and coarse.

Yet, gentle were those rough and work-scarred hands:
gentle His hands of blessing on little children's heads,
gentle His fingers on eyes long blind,
and gentle His touching of the deaf mute's ears and tongue.
Oh, potent was the hand of pity that raised
the demon-stricken boy from torment
and Jairus' daughter from her childhood bed of death;
quick the loving hand that lifted stricken Peter from the waves;
priestly the hands that broke communion bread and passed the cup;
kind the hand of reprimand that mended Malchus' ear;
and patient were the punctured hands that Thomas touched—
those coarse and gentle craftsman's hands,
made ugly by the rarest comeliness of love.

## *Solomon Sky*

*Proverbs 16:18\**

Swift tumults of the wind abrade
proud clouds that flaunt themselves on high.
Oh, grandly did these clouds parade
(like puffed-up ghosts) across the sky,
till whirling, heaving, hidden wind
brought to a thin and empty end
the pageant of their grey charade,
and only drifting wisps abide
where once high rode the bloat of pride.

*\*Pride goeth before destruction, and an haughty spirit before a fall.*

## *Counterparts*

Unless assailed by fear
or eager for a treat
from dog-loving neighbors,
Oliver walks in easy obedience on a short leash—
until we approach the last corner of our walk.
Inevitably, then, he tugs and scrambles to our left,
insisting that we will, indeed,
round the corner for home.

I give him a gracious longer leash until the turn,
thankful that as I approach my final corner,
sometimes tugging at the leash of grace,
the Master's grip, indeed, will guide me home.

# *Psychology 101*

*Remembering with delight people like
Buddy Hackett and Jimmy Durante*

### Lesson for the Day

| | |
|---|---|
| The face of Mr. A. | The face of Mr. B. |
| supports an ugly nose. | thrusts forth a peak-like beak. |
| The charm of Mr. A. | The self of Mr. B. |
| envelops him like clothes. | is graceless, mean, and weak. |
| And so from day to day, | No charm in him we see; |
| no matter what some say, | his company we flee— |
| we love the nose of Mr. A. | and loathe the nose of Mr. B. |

### One-Sentence Summary for the Test

Wherever we may find it,
we come to love or loathe
a spiked or bloated nose
for what we find behind it.

## *The Victim*

Pity the feminist university lecturer,
passionately disseminating her anti-masculine views,
holding seminar upon seminar—
without knowing
    the potent history
    of that word.

## *Partly Subliminal*

My narrow memory of grade five brings up
Ray Krone, whose parentage was mysterious,
who manufactured and retailed naughty stories,
and who sang the alto part when the teacher asked
us to sing stanzas of hymns together.
And I relish the memory of the British newcomer,
Kenneth Button, who always wore knickers
and used British phrases like "I say, old chap!" and "jolly good."

But the classroom has slipped into mist—
except for one wondrous day,
likely the first day of the year.
On that day Mrs. Hoekstra gave each of us
a shiny new geography book.
I recall the pictures and the glossy paper,
and I remember the mystery and the marvel of Malaya.
Most clearly I remember the scent of the book—
not the usual musty, closet scent of textbooks
that reeked of age and sticky hands,
but the sleek, smooth scent of clean paper and fresh ink.

That scent lingers in my memory,
and the memory of that scent
brings a sense of childhood quiet and comfort,
a sense that things are all right,
an unconsidered childhood sense that
my little world is protected by a circle of security,
security of parents and of home,
of teachers in school,
of good people in church,
and—as they taught with unpretentious love and faith—
the security of God.
Is this, perhaps, odd?
Yes, and real.

## *Accessory to the Crimes*

My friend in grades eight and nine
stole red packs of Pall Mall cigarettes from the gas station.
As we spent our afternoons in the woods,
we smoked and felt mildly unrighteous, at best—
I, the accessory to the theft,
tacitly laying the moral burden on him,
and he smugly affecting carelessness.
We never talked about it.

After the first few times
our smoking was no longer experimental.
We did not inhale the smoke, except by unhappy accident,
and though I loathed the taste of tobacco,
I masked my loathing with manly pretense of pleasure.
We did it because we knew it was wrong,
because of pubescent perverseness—
which included schoolyard boasting.

Neither of us became addicted to nicotine,
but my friend had to spend time
in jail ten years later for his addiction to thievery.

And I?
I had to spend time, also—
imprisoned by the goading guilt of my silence.

## *Cleansing*

Not in haste or roughness,
but thoughtfully and gently,
maybe like a mother
bathing her baby, carefully, tenderly,
lingering with love in drying
as she inspects and admires,
so the kneeling Master washed
the filthy, wandering feet of His beloved twelve,
feet that had turned quickly to Him at His bidding,
feet that had carried those slow of heart and mind
with Him on His holy, dusty journeys
for three years of miracles and mercy,
feet that would forsake Him soon,
fleeing through olive shadows of Gethsemane.

Thoroughly, purposefully
He purged those inconstant feet,
and, drying them with that towel,
looked up to find perplexity in the faces of His friends—
looked up and knew their need, their weakness,
looked up, even, to the faithless face of Judas.

Yet, on Friday, how much greater the cleansing,
when, lifted up in condescending agony
and looking down on all His stained creation,
He willingly, thoroughly, purposefully
purged our filthy, wandering souls
in the baptism of His holy blood.

## *Vexation*

A poem is a thing
that you paw and you fling
as a cat mauls a mouse.
Through your whole mental house
you toss it about,
while you grumble and grouse:
"I shake till I ache,
but how do I make
its insides come out?"

## *The Climb*

The higher I climb
up this ladder of time,

the harder I cling
to the whimsical thing.

I've climbed to such height
that the ground's out of sight,

and winds often whip,
so I tighten my grip—

but there's no place to stop
till I come to the top.

I marvel again
about all that has been;

now time's running out,
and my mind deals with doubt.

I grip rungs and rails
as my strength slowly fails;

my heart yearns for peace
as my soul craves release;

I ask as I climb
through ephemeral time:

*Oh, when comes the view,*
*of the promised things new—*

*the view that one day*
*takes my last breath away?*

## *The Curse*

If I could persuade the radiant azalea
to keep its blossoms all the year,
slip the crimson sunset into my fist,
or fan the fragrance of a locust tree
into my mind—and hold it there,
as the heart holds a fetching melody—
then, perhaps, I could ward off
the haunting, empty ache
inflicted by the ravishing hues
and deliciously beguiling scents
of fleeting, sin-smitten spring.

## *Paradigms*

Pear trees,
nature's prayer candles,
point snow-pure flames of devotion
into the draping
darkness.

## *Like a Duck*

We always *cast* ballots (or aspersions or spells),
and we always *throw* a fit (or a game or a party),

but we never *throw* ballots (or aspersions or spells),
and we never *cast* a fit (or a party or a game).

Language, it seems,
in spite of all its wanton change,
often gets stuck.
It loves spasmodic constancy—
much like a duck.*

*Ducks are seasonally or intermittently monogamous.

### *Flowering Crab*

Tender sprigs tremble,
bowed with dew-laden weight of
fragile, fleeting pink.

## *Faith*

Because I was required to have a heart test before cataract surgery,
I did.

After her review of the cardiogram the gracious doctor said,
"We'll talk."

Then, having listened carefully with her stethoscope at all of my vital points,
she said,

"Well, it's all very good: heart rhythm, rate, and strength are all
just fine."

Then she paused, pointed to the EKG results, and looked directly at
my face.

"But," she said evenly, "according to this, you should be having a heart attack
right now."

Though inexperienced with attacks (even after startling news) I replied,
"I'm not."

"And even to oblige your machine," I thought, "I don't especially
want one."

Well, there was no panic, no re-take, no aspirin to chew, and not even a
wheelchair.

"We'll send the report to your ophthalmologist," said the cheerful receptionist as
I left.

All of that was so refreshingly unscientific that the next day I called to say
thank you.

Shortly after that the ophthalmologist fearlessly performed the surgery on
my eyes.

The book of Hebrews defines faith as "the evidence of things
not seen."

Right now I am wondering who in this story showed the
most faith.

## *Opportunity*

Ringing
the lofty rim
of the old white tower,
vultures struggle for vantage to
eat death.

### *Laughing Buddha*

Omphaloskepsis* requires eyesight,
a navel, and an unobstructed view.

Now, of those rigid three necessities
the jolly, bulging Budai** had but two.

Grinning at his image, one must wonder:
how *did* the sometimes-musing Budai do?

*meditation while gazing at the navel
** the so-called laughing Buddha, pronounced *Boo-die*

## *Cremation after All*

### *A Two-Part Invention*

#### I
*Hartford, Connecticut, 1883*

When Mrs. Clemens took a look
at Twain's new *Mississippi* book,
she viewed with pain and deep concern
the sketch that showed her husband burn
in something like cremation fire.
In fact, the sketch set off her ire,
and Mrs. Clemens undertook
to have Sam strike it from his book.
And so the sketch was soon excised,
and she was pleased because he prized
her love—and Twain, yet in his prime,
postponed cremation for some time.

#### II
*Roseland, Chicago, ca. 1948*

Our three-boy club of boyhood days
exploited well the boyhood phase
of clandestine and harmless deeds—
benign adventures no one heeds:
surveillance of the neighborhood,
(in working for the common good),
long obsequies for Fred's pet fish
(as formal as a fish could wish),
the writing of our fearsome rules,
and close surveillance of the schools.

"Fred! Fred!" I yelled far down the block,
"My bike key fits the school door lock!"
"Be quiet, man. Let's go and see."
So off we went to try the key.
And, yes! it worked. We slipped inside,

discovered places there to hide,
established there our club's new base,
found old oak floors on which to race,
inspected drawers and rooms unknown,
and claimed the place for us alone.

And so we rode a happy crest
and kept our secret from the rest—
from pupils, teachers, principal.
Our covert cup of joy was full.

Alas! the cup turned upside down,
and joy died at my father's frown.
His stern demeanor left no doubt:
authorities had found us out.
"Do you have anything to say?"
he asked. I cringed, fear and dismay
assailing me. "Downstairs!" he said,
"The furnace room." And down I fled.

Awaiting justice, there I stood,
the blazing furnace for my good
brought visions of brave Daniel's friends—
and souls whose torment never ends.
My backside, quivering with fear,
predicted that my fate was near.

Down came my father; in his face
strong purpose showed, but little grace.
His clench of mouth and gleam of eye
made clear that judgement hovered nigh.
His strong decree: our club was dead,
and I (the founder, fountainhead,
and root from which our sins had stemmed)
yes, I was now the one condemned
to cut all ties with both my friends,
since I had led them to bad ends.

Then suddenly I realized
his hand held books that I had prized,
books he had taken from the shelf
of books he read to us himself—
*Tom Sawyer, Huckleberry Finn.*
Those books had led me into sin
my father said. And, saying so,
in order to relieve his woe
and consummate his dreadful ire,
he flung them both into the fire.
The furnace flamed; despite my pain
cremation came at once to Twain.

## *Invasive Species*

Dame's rocket,* phlox-like and invasive,
now abounds in thickets, woods, and ditches,
mixing white and purple-pink in rich abandon.
Brushed by breeze and quickly, lightly stirring,
sweetly it cleans the tranquil evening air
with pure elixir of its luscious scent.
Invasive, yes—and welcome here to vanquish,
occupy, transfix both sense and mind.

Now old pines sigh with evening wind's caress;
somewhere nearby explodes a cardinal's cry.
From pink and white the sacrifice of scent ascends
as Venus, veiled, glides silent down the sky.

---

**Dame's rocket (hesperis matronalis—mother of the west or evening) is a plant frequently mistaken for phlox. It has four petals, not five, as phlox have, and its leaves are staggered or alternate, not growing directly across from one another, as those of the phlox do.*

## *Mountain*

Nick is thirty-three now, father of two, divorced,
a carpenter's son, a carpenter himself in better years.
Once lithe and wiry, agile and sure-footed in framing or roofing,
he curls on the couch now, thin and fragile,
unable and unwilling to work,
his hair and clothes unkempt, his trousers ragged.
His quick and winsome smile is gone,
his bright blue eyes have dulled, his grey skin reeks of tobacco,
his grey life holds no candle of hope or joy.
He huddles there now, ragged in his soul.
Alcohol, marijuana, and tobacco
have been his close companions since teenage years,
but his faithfulness to them has turned their sweetness bitter.

Does he see the bottle and the weed as traitors?
Does he sip and smoke, loathing himself,
yet blaming weed and bottle, as he blames his schoolmates,
for his binges and addictions?
Or is he tired of blaming other people, other things?
Is he tired of thinking about his tattered life,
tired of badgering and burdening his parents,
tired of isolation, confusion, and seizures,
tired of living and ready to rot behind black curtains of oblivion?

Only God knows why Nick is afflicted with brain cancer.
Only God knows why He wanted Nick to live beyond age two,
when his father rescued him from the truck
that slipped into the scum-crusted pond,
making front-page news that night.
Only God has count of the thousands of prayers for him,
and only God knows the day of Nick's reclamation.

So, Nick is our beloved mountain;
a mountain to be moved by our mustard seeds of faith
and made to stand at the verge of the glistening sea.
Freed from clutching bondage and reeking raggedness,
there he will stand in his radiant robe—
straight, smiling, pristine,
and rich in the fragrance of grace.

## *Enticement*

The honey locust wins no prize
for pulchritude of shape or size.
She lacks the grandeur of the oak
and crimson hue of maple's cloak;
her scattered limbs, too thinly spread,
provide scant roundness overhead.
But though without allure she stands,
a potent charm she yet commands;
for from her catkins sweetly drifts
a paragon of nature's gifts:
a fragrance, elegant and pure,
a subtle scent well fit to lure
the passerby to pause and sigh—
to breathe again and quickly try
to catch another wave of scent
that wafts from branches lower bent.

And so this unassuming tree,
this model of sweet modesty,
demurely lures the sense and thought
of those who pass—whose hearts are caught
and for a moment drawn away
by honey locust's soft bouquet.

## Nellie Tibble

My first teacher emerges from my memory,
half hidden in the tumbling twilight of childhood.
Hers was a classroom of four grades,
the children of each grade sitting in a straight row.
I sat last in the first-grade row,
behind the four or five girls in my class,
behind a girl whose locks hung down, enticing, on my desk.

I see Miss Tibble standing before the class, dressed in brown,
and though she is neither tall nor plump,
her height and size impart authority.
Her auburn hair, coming down in tousled curls,
surrounds a face both plain and kind.

Miss Tibble's fiancé died in the war,
and she left the little school in Iowa for New Mexico.
There she taught and sheltered Navaho children
in a log cabin constructed by Navaho Christians
amid the lonesome landscape of the reservation.
And so, in solitude, with small provision, and with slight acclaim,
she served her Master as she served His children.

Enjoying few comforts,
struggling in weariness and fear—
and yet, perhaps, with quiet joy—
she made her modest mark upon this world,
carrying and making known God's shameful mark:
the glorious cross of Christ.

## *Recreation Comes to Michigan*

(*Michigan voters pass "recreational" marijuana initiative*)

The voters have revealed their minds
in action legal that now binds:
we may, it seems, make sport with pot
in games and leagues of many kinds.

So, some are busy hyping pot,
and some inhale it piping hot
so it can oil or boil their brains
to view the world as it is not.

Yes, they will exercise the soul:
quite blithely will they fill the bowl
and gaily pipe strange vapors in,
as merrily as did King Cole.

Now, scientists through research find
that smoking pot will dull the mind.
That's what our voters clearly show
when passing laws of just this kind.

## *The Party Line*

(Creating Caucus in the Classroom)
*A short and hortatory rhyme
concerning education in our time*

The craven crow caws coarsely, queerly.
He caws as if he's daft—or nearly.

His pulpit is a dry cornstalk;
from there he tears the air with squawk,

addressing chicks in birch and pine
with notions from the party line.

These fledglings cannot yet divine
the dangers of the party line,

so every fledgling should be taught
to sort out rhetoric from thought.

If that's a concept you find thin,
just listen to the crow again

and note that with his raucous squawking
it's fledglings' minds this fowl is stalking—

and though you find his squawking raucous,
he could be Churchill to his caucus.

## Homage to "The Red Wheelbarrow"*

Wheelbarrow?
Of course.

Yet much more
depends

on the bright steel
shopping cart

sheathed in weeds
knee-high

beside the
black path.

*"The Red Wheelbarrow," 1923, by William Carlos Williams, imagist poet (1883—1963)

## *A Question for Flag Haters*

On this third of July the sun pours down
through moisture-laden air.
Across our little pond
a colony of sweating shinglers
swarms a condominium building,
working in concord like
purposeful ants or honey bees,
straining on the scorching roof
and scrambling about the lawns
with tarpaulins and plywood,
all of them brown-skinned immigrants,
active, industrious, quick with smiles,
and willing to struggle in the sun
for a long day's wage.

So, if tomorrow they should see
Old Glory, blowing straight and free—
blue sky above and peace beneath—
what hatred will *their* hearts unsheath?

## *Maranatha*

*Come, Lord*

    To the god that was no god
some of God's people burned their infants in Hinnom—
offered them there in Gehenna to the molten, fire-belching arms
of Molech's hideous image, while deafening drums
and ceremonial screams covered the infants' shrieks of agony.
        Urns of tiny immolated skulls and bones remain.

    For a cause that was no cause
Nazis murdered Jews in gas chambers,
incinerated some of their corpses in furnaces,
and dumped bones and ashes into common graves, ponds, or rivers,
hoping to cover both infamy and agony from the world's notice.
        Urns of commingled ashes went in falsehood to relatives of some.

    For a reason that has no reason
white-coated operatives slice or crush our infants in the womb,
burn their dismembered bodies,
sell severed parts for profit,
and cover both infamy and agony under pretext.
        Garbage cans or boxes carry mutilated babies to their fiery end.

    Humans who are not human
kneel to the kindler of Molech's flames,
the igniter of Nazi hate, the inciter of abortionist fervor—
the demonic source of every ghastly perversion.
*How long, oh Lord, how long until your justice*
        *binds him deep within Gehenna's quenchless flames?*

## West Ward

*Pine Rest, 1955\**

Locking the door behind us,
we paused in the dark, heavy-smelling room,
lit feebly by a tiny, naked bulb in the ceiling.
"\_\_\_ \_\_\_\_\_ you for livin'!" bellowed a voice
from the first bed on our left.
The man lay on his back in catatonic posture,
his head elevated without a pillow.
In spite of the seasoned attendant with me,
the man was eager to intimidate a new orderly.
Feisty he was and fearsome,
reputed to hoist his bed above his head.

I had come across the way from the Children's Retreat,
having for the first stint of my night shift
helped to put youngsters to bed:
some compulsive or stubborn,
some troubled and angry,
some uncomprehending and sweet.

Now I stood in Building One, West Ward,
the communal residence of disturbed, even violent male patients,
a dark place where pain and compassion were supposed to meet.
We walked through the odorous gloom
down the aisle that separated two long rows of beds—
my place of work for nights to come.
There they lay, victims of confusion,
compulsion, despair, delusion, rage,
and agony of mind and body,
some having forgotten hope,
some, perhaps, never having known it.
I was to be the supervisor of their sleep,
their helper to the bathroom,
their bringer of peace in stress or strife,
the changer of their bedclothes and mopper of their messes.

Toward the end of my tenure in West Ward
I learned of a therapy for the violently disturbed: the *pack sheet*.
When I came on duty, a patient of just my age
had been wrapped tightly in the long, damp sheet
and was agonizing in one of the padded cells outside the ward.
Peering through the small square in the thick door,
I saw the boy on a cot, the very semblance of a mummy,
unable to move and cursing in the anguish of desperation.
Seeing my face, he tried to spit through the opening.
Compassion overcoming my fear and revulsion,
I unlocked the heavy door and came beside him
with words as my only weapon against his agony.
But whatever they were, the words were useless,
for the distracted boy struggled to find his pillow with his teeth
and viciously attempted to fling it at me.

Looking through the little window in memory's door,
I can still view the horror of that constriction,
I can still feel the terror and rage of helplessness;
and as I turn from the window, I still must ask,
why was *I* the one looking in?

*Pine Rest Christian Mental Health Services, Grand Rapids, Michigan, was founded in 1910 by the Reformed Church in America and the Christian Reformed Church in America. Until 1952 it was called Christian Psychopathic Hospital.

## *Handicapped*

Sometimes our church choir went to sing
for the evening service at the Pine Rest chapel.
As we sat quietly waiting,
patients tramped up the entrance steps
or clattered in from the ramp for the handicapped.
Eager they seemed and happy to come,
maybe pleased by the change of routine
or happy because they liked singing—
or because they felt comfort and strength within God's building.

Pastor Vander Laan arose to begin the service,
walking confidently with his white cane.
He spoke with slightly-lifted head,
as if sensing the presence of the Spirit.
Soon he invited the patients to pray,
and one by one they came to talk to God.
Pastor Jim stood close to each one, holding the microphone
for the simple prayers, for the words that halted or tumbled
from the mouths and hearts of struggling souls.
Patiently he stood,
never interrupting the mumbled, the obscure,
or the rambling prayers of God's children.

How clear it became then, the truth about impairment.
We were one: the struggling patients, the sightless pastor,
and the rest of us, flawed and small—all somehow handicapped—
and yet each one made plumb and perfect
by the Cornerstone of God's great edifice of grace.

### *Petunias Bunched in the Sidewalk Crack*

In one row
    unsown
they grow.
Overnight
    they came;
purple-white
they bloom,
    ignoring
doom,
content
    with place,
and bent
to face
    the sun
with grace—
until
    raw frost
will chill
their bloom
    or accident
will doom
their beauty—
    end their hidden
duty.

## *Pine Rest Chapel, 1929—2019*\*

*A Lament*

Red bricks, grey concrete buttresses and arches,
dark wooden beams, Victorian stained glass, plaster and paint,
an oak floor and pews, a pulpit on a platform:
together these insensate objects formed a place
where the pain-stricken, the confused, the empty
could come to take new breath for their struggles.

This was no mere meeting room, no common hall.
This was an enclosure of peace, a place of modest beauty,
a refuge from wards and beds and hospital regimens,
a place where the organ sounded and the chaplain spoke,
where patients sang and prayed—
a place with God at the center.

Today, behind these bands of yellow tape
lies a heap of rubble wrought by crane and bulldozer:
scattered bricks and bent steel beams, shattered roof and walls,
tangled conduits, stained and stinking ceiling tiles,
and two grey, mutilated organ pipes,
lying silent astride the debris of the toppled tower.

Almost a century ago devoted women\*\*
stitched and canned and prayed for the making of this chapel.
Ninety years ago both architect and builders
shaped a vision into pleasing symmetry.
Erected by labor and by love, this building served
to enclose the sick and the simple with peace.

But here the handiwork of holy cause
lies crushed and will be carted to the dump;
this sacred place will be an empty lawn—
as empty as the heart for gifts of grace
and winsome beauty now for all time gone.

*The chapel was closed about 2007. It was allowed to deteriorate until its destruction in July, 2019.

**The cornerstone indicated that the chapel was built with money given by women's circles of Christian Psychopathic Hospital (re-named Pine Rest in 1952).

## *Liz*

*Lynden, early 1950's*

Seated on benches surrounding the bed of the old covered truck,
we had jostled to the farm to pick pole beans.
Liz was heavyset, so perhaps that is why she jumped down last.
Turning to the field, no one thought much about Liz—
until we heard her shriek, "Mamma! Mamma!"
Turning back, we saw her bend in distorted agony—
and then we saw her torn-off finger in the dust.
Looking up, we saw the nail that caught her ring.

A nail, a ring—
and every bean, it seemed,
a finger.

## *Sundown*

In deep evening's hush
    tall trees stretch shadows,
        black across the sun-green lawn.

*Those verdant years,*
    *those fresh and verdant years,*
        *soon, oh, how soon have they gone.*

## Tree Huggers

*De gustibus non disputandum est.\**

Tree frogs
cling to trees,
and when August comes,
one clings to another
to produce more
tree frogs
that cling to trees
and (if they are males) buzz out long, monotonous songs
in order to attract females
in order to produce even more
tree frogs.
To do that they find water
on the ground or in leaves
because the eggs need water
because the eggs are fertilized
outside the female's body
because—
but let's omit the clinical,
because no one ever sees
a single tree frog, anyway,
let alone an oddly copulative couple.
You can't miss the song, though—
but you know that if the human male
ever rasped and buzzed amours
in that prolonged monotone,
the buzzing would produce nothing more
than a genuine female headache.
Of course, beauty is in the ear of the listener,
so who are we to question the innate taste
of the female tree hugger
who craves the cold clasp of a moist male hugger
whose nocturnal passion emits those buzz saw buzzings
through dozens and dozens of sultry summer nights?

\*"Concerning taste there is no dispute"—an ancient Latin sentence of obscure origin.

## *Sunflower Field I*

*II Corinthians 4:6\**

The red-winged blackbird
rasps a prelude from a patch
of thistles in the ditch
while the congregation of ten thousand stands,
golden faces lifted to the east.

Regal, resplendent,
the pastor mounts with dignity his celestial pulpit.
Transfixed, his flock adores the splendor of his risen face.
Not a whisper wafts across the field,
no disrupting rustle mars the burning sermon.
The black-backed cricket checks its song;
wild peppermint holds its scented breath.
Wholly heliotropic\*\* is this congregation:
every face turns east to feast
on the fiercely-burning countenance
that beams down golden gifts of life and peace.
Heliotropic, holy is this flock,
earthly, unearthly a paradigm of true worship
and radical religion.

*\*For God, who commanded light to shine out of darkness,*
*hath shined in our hearts,*
*to give the light of the knowledge*
*of the glory of God*
*in the face of Jesus Christ.*

*\*\*heliotropic: turning with the sun*

## *South End Reporter*

*Roseland, Chicago, c. 1947*

Once a week we walked the mile to our paper route,
trudged to another neighborhood,
where the papers awaited us on the curb.
Once there, we rolled them up, hundreds of them,
stuffed them into our bags, and staggered up and down the sidewalks
to bless the residents with the contents
of the *South End Reporter*.
Once each month we went to do the collecting,
my older brother, Gaylord, and I.
Ten cents we collected from each customer;
three cents we might keep
for the pleasure of purveying intellectual nourishment.
Up and down the streets we went,
children in a neighborhood not our own.
Sometimes we waited on the porches,
and sometimes we went into houses.
    "How much is it again?
    A dime? I'll be right back."
Up and down we went
inside the red brick two-flats and three-flats
with their dark hallways and reeking apartments.
We hurried to get out sometimes, but we never had trouble,
and usually we came out with the necessary dimes.
And when the hours and the task had passed,
off we went to the nearby clapboard grocery store,
where each of us lavished ten cents of our earnings
on a tall bottle of Royal Crown Cola and a bag of potato chips.
Kings we were then, throned on the curb in front of that old store,
pockets bulging with coins and stomachs with fizz.

## *The Shade*

*Matthew 6:34\**

How comfortable the darkness of deception,
when our psyches draw down for us protecting shades.
Thus, the ceaseless smoker defies lung cancer,
the hard drinker mocks addiction,
and the stock car racer winks at accidents.
Visiting my ancient, feeble, pain-stricken friends,
without thought I also draw down an opaque shade,
blocking the prospect that one day I will sit,
chair-bound, drooling, and staring at my lap,
perhaps without hearing or memory,
maybe aching in my bones and brain,
anguished, maybe, with visions of times both sweet and free,
those years of usefulness, of vigor, and of clarity,
of making music in my mind and with my hands,
of bicycling or walking or drinking tea with friends.

But still, I will not seek to raise my shade.
Unlike the shades of some, it is a gift,
a friend and helper to obedience:
it lets tomorrow fret about itself.

*\*Take therefore no thought for the morrow;*
*for the morrow shall take thought for the things of itself.*

## *Invitation*

*Matthew 11:28*

He who walked through Israel,
twice homeless, having nowhere to lay His head,
maybe nostalgic for Nazareth, homesick for heaven,
languishing in holy lonesomeness
as the pestilence of sin pressed Him on every side,
empty for heaven's pristine fellowship with His Father,
scorned, shunned, forsaken by His followers,
alone before Pilate, and, fastened to the ghastly tree,
in utmost extremity abandoned even by His Father—
that Lonesome One, that Homesick One,
in Galilee one day held out His hands
to hearts heavy-laden with soul-searing lonesomeness,
to hearts empty with unknown homesickness for heaven—
held out his hands and said in heaven's way of paradox,
"Come unto me;
*I* will give you rest."

## *Suitability*

When I was just a sprouting lad,
we went to church sedately clad.
We called the clothes we wore then "Sunday,"
since few of us dressed up for Monday.
The women wore both hats and skirts;
the men wore suits and well-starched shirts.
The children, clad in suits and frocks,
in Sunday shoes and Sunday socks,
sat still until their minds grew dull
(or till they squirmed from scratchy wool).
Then peppermints, dispensed by Dad,
were all the sustenance they had
to get them through the three-point sermon,
long as Jordon, high as Hermon.
Had someone lost his calendar,
the clothes we wore would make it clear:
this was the first day of the week,
and, though our dress need not be chic,
our time of worship still required
that we be suitably attired.

Capricious are our clothing ways,
for they are quite reversed these days.
Now Sunday best gets sabbath rest.
It waits for us to be well-dressed
on weekdays when we need aplomb
for wedding, interview, or prom;
and, worn by coaches at the games,
it satisfies some hidden aims.

Though Sunday garb gets sabbath rest,
we should not fret or grow distressed.
Some sage this wisdom might impart:
"We worship not with clothes but heart,
and every thinking person knows
that hearts have no clear link to clothes."

## *Crescent Moon Rising*

The goal of science is to lay things bare.
The misty, yellow moon, arising there
with mystery and sweet suggestive power,
for us one day slight mystery will hold;
for scientists will measure, map, and scour
till all its secrets have been plainly told.
Will then our fancy and our joy grow cold,
as when the warty facts of brain and frame
snuff out from love the mystique—and the flame?

## *Ecclesiastical Cricket*

Ecclesiastes 3:11*

Easy it is for us, craving sleep,
to loathe the creaking cricket,
who sends his drilling monotone into the night
from his tiny, hidden thicket;
and easy it is for us, waking,
to delight in the lyric finch,
who weaves a wispy wreath of song
from the nearby purple-leaved crab tree.

Though we might wish the crusty cricket
to sing with finch-like sweetness,
how lonesome his existence if, indeed,
some sweet and silvery song replaced
the scraping and unbroken croaking monotone
with which he woos and welcomes his reluctant bride.

And so, the Preacher—knowing as he did
the screaming of jackals and the rumbling of pachyderms,
knowing lyric songbirds' songs
and long laments of forlorn loons—
learned as he was,
maybe also knew the beauty that imbues
the insistent cricket's courting cry—
knew its ugly beauty in God's resplendent tapestry
of time and place and need.

*He hath made everything beautiful in his time.*

## *The Unfathomable Theology of Fishing*

"I want to leave this world," said Cliff,
who at age ninety struggles with pain,
with loss of hearing and memory,
and with the death of his wife, Lynn.
"I came close a couple of times.
Why can't I go now?"

I said, "I can't tell you."
Cliff struggles with guilt
and getting right with God, so I added,
"Maybe God is giving you time to grow—
maybe in faith, or assurance, or knowledge."

Cliff shifted into metaphor.
"Well," he said, "I think He caught me
 and threw me back a couple of times."

I laughed roundly, and Cliff smiled.
(Metaphor is hardly his mode.)

I didn't ask what fishing gear God had used,
but when I visit Cliff again, I'll say that
God is almost certainly on His next expedition,
carrying a clean, shiny hook
and a deep, unbreakable net.

## *Royce*

Empty for the fifth night is the long red pickup truck,
its covered bed crammed with unknown possessions.
Yes, empty without Royce, crowded behind the wheel,
taking in the night air through the open window,
and enjoying his freedom,
as he did waking and sleeping for many months.

I peer into the interior of cab,
just to be sure, and again I see
plastic bags, debris, a hat, a shirt or jacket—
and I leave the truck, tucked lonesome under drooping trees
in the dark back corner of the parking lot behind the library.

I resume my walk towards home,
but I cannot outwalk the image of the empty cab;
nor can I escape the thought that
maybe this time Royce is finally gone,
gone from his truck home, gone from the hospitals
to a bright new home—
>without a failing heart
>and bleeding, festering legs,
>without cancer in his colon
>and the ugliness of his illnesses,
>without memories of war, dying daughters,
>and lonesomeness and poverty,
>without devilish pain and doctors and ambulance rides
>and wondering about tomorrow's food.

He would have made a classic Santa Claus
with his white beard, his rubicund and genial face,
his twinkling eye and rotund frame.
His gifts? An instant smile, a hearty handclasp,
and lessons in good cheer and pliant patience.
Never did he question God's ways;
never was he abject or bitter or hopeless.

Always he looked with eagerness toward his bright new home,
especially, it seemed, after his baptism last year in the nearby lake.
Maybe he has reached that home now,
liberated from the freedom he sought in his cab prison,
gone forever from that very full, very empty red truck,
now lonesome under drooping trees
in the dark back corner of the parking lot.

## *Robinical Example*

*Philippians 3:13,14\**

Leaving behind the struggles of mating and nesting,
forgetting the respite of sunny summer branches,
silent, south-bound robins
fly swift and straight, tree to tree.
No urge just now for even a fragment of song.
No time now, it seems, for hopping about
and worrying worms beneath the leaf-laden lawns.
Time only to pluck shrinking crab apples—
sudden strength for pressing on with the arduous flight.

*\* . . . but this one thing I do, forgetting the things that are behind . . . I press toward the mark for the prize of the high calling of God in Jesus Christ."*

## *Sunflower Field II*

Gone is their rapture of gold,
gone the splendor of their sun-turned faces.
Each blackened face hangs feeble
under grey and layered skies,
hangs lonely with the standing dead—
the concentration camp of feeble stems,
dry—dry and brown, some broken at the neck,
unable to sustain the weight of faded radiance.
Every black, impassive face stares steadfastly down,
down toward its dark place of destiny.

Pleasing it is to ponder the fancy that
in some deep fiber of their dying selves
they sense the mighty strength of seed and sun
and hold within their desiccated depths
the potent hope of resurrection gold.

## One by One

*A thought as Teresa Herrema's life ends*

One by one waves search the shore,
collecting stones and shells and more.
One by one to sea they go,
helpless in strong undertow—
    into the grey, mysterious sea
    that bears each to eternity.

No power nor plan can they command
to hold their place upon the strand.
Strength unrelenting draws them all,
one by one—the great, the small—
    into the vast, mysterious sea
    that borders bright eternity.

### *Avian Diplomacy*

Birds
define their spheres
with song.

How
can such technique
be wrong?

### *Arroyo* *

Grief is
an arroyo,
dry, empty, awaiting
the next tumultuous torrent
of tears.

*arroyo: a dry gully, quickly filled with rushing water from higher ground*

## Dwelling Place

All-comprehending Dove—
in our small thoughts celestially white,
in Your holy being, pure and perfect—
You occupy the deepest caverns of my mind,
You permeate minute recesses of my flesh,
and with Your purging, re-creating flame
You shape from deep depravity and dust
     a temple for Yourself.

And yet that temple grows but slowly,
and often at Your love I wonder:
     how can it be
     that daily You
     abide in me?
    Indeed, how can it be
    that my proximity
    makes no befouling spot,
    leaves no polluting blot
    upon Your purity?

Strong Spirit, take no corded whip, no scourge,
but springing water take, with hyssop* purge,
and of this temple make a pristine space,
one fit and spotless for your dwelling place.

*hyssop: a plant, the leaves of which are pressed to make oil for cleansing*

## *November Rose*

November rose,
you blossomed first in June,
and summer's sun
you knew, and August moon.

October's frost
your ruby petals bore;
you budded still,
and still you blossomed more.

And now cruel snows
have caused your stems to bend;
but they, like love,
hold beauty to the end.

## *Immanuel*

Two thousand years ago
God assumed our flesh and lived with us.
Two thousand years ago
Jesus promised His perpetual presence.

    Now, each December, looking to Christmas Day,
    we read the prophecies in church and light candles,
    pretending that Jesus must still be born.
    During the week we use the holy birth
    to justify exhaustive shopping and lavish giving,
    as well as to give reason for lights, decorations, and parties.
    Ceaseless carols and glitzy Christmas music
    provide relentless shopping background,
    and Santa, Rudolph, and elves
    favor the season with their fairytale presence—
    even when Providence withholds
    the emotional necessity of snow.

Two thousand years ago
Zacharias uttered blessing,
Mary exclaimed praise,
the shepherds rejoiced,
Mary mused on the holy wonders,
Simeon blessed God,
and Anna offered thanks.
That was all:

    no parties, lights, or decorations.
    Even the ecstatic Magi shunned thin festivities
    when the marvelous star brought them at last
    to Jesus with their precious gifts and adoration.

Well, of course, they had the real Christmas, the real Jesus.
We have mere manger scenes and creches,
and we simply need to make the best of it.
So, we strive to make Christmas—
what's the Hallmark word?—*special*.

Does God understand our Advent make-believe,
our expecting of Immanuel, already with us?
And does He smile at our tinsel Christmases?
Comforting it is that our patient Immanuel bears with us—
even during our sometimes odd observations,
our sometimes thin, synthetic celebrations,
and, let us hope, our blatant desecrations
of His holy nativity.

## *Addiction*

Carefully, deliberately,
you sharpen your new pencil
until its point feels firm and needle-like.
Pleased with its readiness, you take it up
and eagerly begin a fresh page.
Despite your every care and caution,
its fragile point snaps,
marring the clean, new page
with an ugly, unerasable smudge.
And then, lips set tight,
in trembling retribution
you grasp the broken tool
and fill that tainted page with
fierce and mindless scrawls.

## *Ocular Oxymoron*

Sad it was, indeed,
 to learn that my neighbor
had a serious eye problem.
So, I tried not to smile
when he gravely affirmed
his affliction to be
"immaculate degeneration."

As I consider it, though,
that might be the best kind.

## *Solace at Solstice*

*A Winter Hymn*

Silent, invisible,
the mighty machinery
that moves this earth—
    prodigious its workings,
    minutely precise
    strictly predictable.
How marvelous is that machinery—
and how comforting.

## *Seasonal Spirit*

*An observation for
January 6 or so*

Christmas is the time of peace,
when joy and light make sweet increase—
till, holding back an inward frown,
you take its outworn trappings down.
Just then you spy a nameless box,
not right for shirt or tie or sox—
an empty box with no clear use
that gives no hint of scents or spruce—
a box that says when you come near it,
"I hold the priceless Christmas spirit.
My contents grow and shrink with time
and change from bleak to hope sublime.
You'll place me high upon the shelf
with tree and star and creche and elf,
and there I'll stay and grow quite spare;
but, come next Christmas, I'll be there."
So, cheered, you close the closet door,
reflecting, as you end your chore:
"All's well: it's safe up on shelf
with tree and star and creche and elf."

And so it goes from year to year
with peace and light and Christmas cheer.

## *Transport*

### *A Waking Dream*

Strong angel, swiftness from God,
holy helper at my bright new birth,
sudden, glorious is this flight.
Swift angel, strength from God,
from melting space and tired time
you bear me safely to the City,
where I in trembling ecstasy
shall know the Holy Presence.
Gone at last is earth-bound yearning,
gone demonic doubt, gone itching sin;
for rapture now surpasses rapture,
and only crystal peace surrounds our going.

www.ingramcontent.com/pod-product-compliance
Lightning Source LLC
Chambersburg PA
CBHW071744040426
42446CB00012B/2465